eco GUIDES

A Teen Guide to

Eco-Leisure

Neil Morris

Heinemann
LIBRARY
Chicago, Illinois

Edited by Andrew Farrow, Adam Miller, and Vaarunika Dharmapala
Designed by Richard Parker
Original illustrations © Capstone Global Library Ltd 2013
Illustrated by HL Studios
Picture research by Tracy Cummins
Originated by Capstone Global Library Ltd
Printed and bound in China by CTPS

16 15 14 13 12
10 9 8 7 6 5 4 3 2 1

Library of Congress Cataloging-in-Publication Data
Morris, Neil.
  A teen guide to eco-leisure / Neil Morris.
    p. cm.—(Eco guides)
  Includes bibliographical references and index.
  ISBN 978-1-4329-7047-5 (hb)—ISBN 978-1-4329-7052-9 (pb) 1. Teenagers and the environment. 2. Leisure—Environmental aspects. I. Title.

  GE195.M668 2013
  304.2—dc23   2012009965

Acknowledgments

We would like to thank the following for permission to reproduce photographs: Alamy p. 8 (© Gavin Hellier); Capstone Library p. 20 (Karon Dubke); Corbis p. 5 (© Tom Bol/Aurora Photos), 10 (© Darren Kemper), 14 (© Tomas Rodriguez), 22 (© David Burton/Beateworks), 26 (© Mika), 32 (© Atlantide Phototravel); Getty Images pp. 7 (Fabrice Dimier/Bloomberg), 13 (TORSTEN BLACKWOOD/AFP), 23 (Mike Harrington), 28 (Blend Images/Moxie Productions), 35 (Lee Strickland), 36 (Andersen Ross), 45 (Laurence Monneret), 46 (altrendo images); istockphoto pp. 42 (© iztok noc), 49 (© Jennifer Byron); Newscom pp. 31 (TELAM Xinhua News Agency), 40 (David Barnes/ DanitaDelimont.com "Danita Delimont Photography"); Shutterstock pp. 4 (Ryan Rodrick Beiler), 9 (Undergroundarts.co.uk), 12 (Volodymyr Goinyk), 15 (Perry Harmon), 16 (Lana K), 17 (John Kasawa), 18 (Darko Zeljkovic), 19 (Lowe Llaguno), 25 (Anatoliy Samara), 27 (Roman Sotola), 29 (rehoboth foto), 30 (Hallgerd), 34 (Ipatov), 37, 39 (l i g h t p o e t), 43 (JustASC); Superstock p. 33 (© Jim West/ age footstock).

Cover photograph of young couple in woodland reproduced with permission of Corbis (© Juice Images). Cover logo reproduced with permission of Shutterstock (Olivier Le Moal).

Every effort has been made to contact copyright holders of material reproduced in this book. Any omissions will be rectified in subsequent printings if notice is given to the publisher.

All the Internet addresses (URLs) given in this book were valid at the time of going to press. However, due to the dynamic nature of the Internet, some addresses may have changed, or sites may have changed or ceased to exist since publication. While the author and publisher regret any inconvenience this may cause readers, no responsibility for any such changes can be accepted by either the author or the publisher.

Contents

Some words are shown in bold, **like this**. You can find out what they mean by looking in the glossary.

Important!
Please check with an adult before doing the projects in this book.

Why Be Green?

Leisure is important to all of us. It is the free time we use to enjoy ourselves. What about eco-leisure? Well, the word *eco* is short for "ecology"—the scientific study of how living things relate to each other and their surroundings. So, eco-leisure involves doing things in your spare time that are helpful to the environment. This could mean recycling junk, saving energy, or getting involved in local projects. You can do all these things and still enjoy your free time. In fact, being green can help you get more pleasure from your leisure!

So, what does "going green" mean?

Since the early 1970s, the word *green* has been used to mean "environmental" or "environmentally friendly." This use of the word originally came from the color's links with grass and plants. If you "go green," you try to live your life in a way that does as little harm as possible to the environment. This includes all Earth's land and sea, as well as the air that we breathe.

In 1971, a small group of environmentalists started an organization called Greenpeace. It has become an influential, international movement. Today, many people around the world call for action on **climate change**.

Plastic versus paper bags

- Paper is from a **renewable** source—managed forests. Plastic is from nonrenewable oil.
- It takes nearly four times more energy and twenty times more water to manufacture a paper bag than to make a plastic one.
- Manufacturing paper and plastic causes acid rain and water pollution.
- It takes 91 percent less energy to recycle a pound of plastic than a pound of paper. But people recycle more paper than plastic.
- Both are bad news in **landfill** sites, because they are slow to **degrade** and give off methane.

So, which is greener? Well, in a word … neither! Reusable bags are best, such as those made from canvas.

Making a start

Don't let difficult eco-decisions intimidate you. The best way to start going green is by taking one step at a time. For example, you could reuse plastic and paper bags until they are falling apart. Then you could put them in the recycling bin and get yourself a reusable bag.

Setting goals

A way to get started on being green in your leisure time is to set yourself some goals and not try to do too much at once. You could look through this book and list some ideas you want to follow. Check off the list items as you put them into action.

Why should I care?

Human life is dependent on the planet on which we live. We need its air to breathe, its water to drink, and its plants to eat. So, it makes sense to take care of Earth. If we ruin it, we will all suffer the consequences. We must also think of future generations.

But what's in it for me?

There are lots of personal advantages to being green. One is that you can save money. Think about two aspects of green living. The first is goods. Do you really need a new cell phone or a new gadget? Resisting the latest trends can save you money, and also damage the world around you less. You could ask yourself questions, as on the flowchart below. You might want a gadget, but do you really need it? If so, and you think you can afford it, you could check this by doing the math. How long do you think the new gadget will last? How much will it cost per month? Are you sure it is better than the old one or worth it at all?

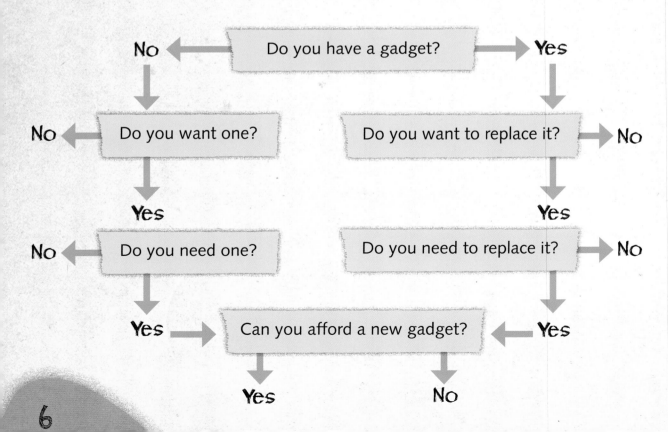

Saving energy and money

Then there is energy use. If you save on heating by putting on an extra sweater, or on electricity by switching things off, the person who pays the bill will face a much smaller charge. Admittedly, this might mean more to your parents than it does to you, but your family will save money. When you are older and pay the bills yourself, you will be used to saving energy and money.

Why me? What about others?

It won't just be your family members who value your green contribution. Teachers and employers see awareness of green issues as an important aspect of everyone's education. So, your green experience could help you get the sort of career you want. It might also matter to your friends, who would much rather hang out with a thoughtful person than a thoughtless one. You won't be alone, and you might find that there are local green groups or projects to join.

Companies bring out new models of their products, such as this iPad, all the time. The latest gadgets can be hard to resist, but do you really need them?

Combating climate change

Global warming and the resulting climate change are the most serious environmental problems facing the world today. Our planet's average global temperature has changed over millions of years, but in the 20th and early 21st centuries, human activities have caused rising temperatures. They have added to the "greenhouse effect," which prevents heat from escaping from Earth, in a similar way to glass trapping warmth inside a greenhouse.

Certain gases in the atmosphere, such as carbon dioxide (CO_2) and methane, cause the effect. We have been adding to these by emitting them from power plants, factories, and cars.

What's a carbon footprint?

We all have our own **carbon footprint**, which means the amount of carbon dioxide (CO_2) each of us produces in our daily lives. Most of this carbon **emission** comes through burning **fossil fuels** (coal, gas, and oil). In more economically developed parts of the world, energy use at home makes up about 27 percent of each person's carbon footprint. Private transportation makes up 10 percent, and public transportation makes up 3 percent. Leisure accounts for 14 percent of our total footprint. This includes emissions caused through the manufacture, delivery, and disposal of products and services we buy.

Eco impact

This table shows the average person's carbon footprint in different countries. The figure is in tons of CO_2 per year.

Australia	20.8
Belize	1.5
Canada	18.1
China	5.8
Germany	10.6
India	1.7
Japan	10.5
Mali	0.1
Qatar	59
Russia	13.3
South Africa	9.7
United Kingdom	9.4
United States	19.3

The 1.9 million people of Qatar, in the Middle East, have the world's biggest average carbon footprint. They use enormous amounts of electricity, especially on air conditioning. This is the night skyline of Qatar's capital, Doha.

By the way, a ton of CO_2 gas is enough to fill nearly 34,000 party balloons.

So, how big is *your* carbon footprint?

You can find carbon calculators on the Internet:

- United States: epa.gov/climatechange/emissions/ind_calculator.html
- Australia: carbonneutral.com.au/carbon-calculator.html

The calculator will ask you questions about your home, your appliances, and your travel. At the end of the questionnaire, you will get your result.

Which of the following do you currently recycle at home?

	YES	NO
NEWSPAPERS?	☐	☐
MAGAZINES?	☐	☐
GLASS?	☐	☐
ALUMINUM AND TIN CANS?	☐	☐
PLASTIC?	☐	☐

How much can you achieve?

The ideas in this book will help you minimize your carbon footprint—but don't forget, it is not about trying to reduce to zero. It is still worth being greener, even if you cannot be totally green. Choose the ideas that you find attractive and goals you think you can achieve. Set up a plan and reward for yourself when you achieve your target.

Carbon offsetting

You might like to try to be "carbon neutral"—that is, a zero CO_2-producer. This is virtually impossible for most people, but there are many companies that offer a solution called carbon offsetting. Every time you fly or go on a long car journey, you calculate the amount of carbon your journey will generate. Then you pay a little extra money on your fare or fuel cost to a company that invests in a green project. This might be an alternative energy program or a new recycling plant, and many programs have government backing. In theory, this offsets (makes up for) the carbon emission your journey caused. Some people like the system, but others think it is just a green con.

The three Rs

One of the easiest ways to start your green career is to follow the three Rs: Reduce, Reuse, and Recycle. These simple R-rules will help you make a green contribution right away by producing less waste, and they can all fit in with your leisure time. Reducing means cutting down on waste by using less in the first place. We can also use things again instead of just throwing them away. We can also recycle, so a new product can be made out of something that has been used before. This is much easier if your home has its recycling collected by a local government program.

If there is no recycling collection in your local area, find your nearest recycling centers.

Starting points

Here are some ideas for getting into the three Rs:

Reducing	• Buy products that use less packaging. • Don't buy more clothes than you need. • Use reusable containers.
Reusing	• Redecorate shoeboxes to store pens, pencils, and drawings. • Avoid **disposable** plates, napkins, cutlery, and batteries. • Cut, flatten, and reuse wrapping paper, envelopes, string, and ribbons.
Recycling	• Buy products made with recycled materials, such as paper and notepads. • Sort trash into groups for recycling: paper and cardboard, glass, metal, and plastic. • Take old shoes and clothes to your local recycling center. • Use fruits and vegetable waste to make compost (plant fertilizer).

Eco impact

- Making one ton of recycled paper saves an average of 17 trees. That is enough to make about 700 phone books, and it saves enough energy to heat an average home for a year.
- It takes three times as much energy to make a new plastic bottle as it does to make a recycled one.
- Recycling one plastic bottle saves enough energy to power a lightbulb for 6 hours.

Three more Rs...

Here are three more Rs to help your new green lifestyle:

- *Rethink*: Ask yourself if you really need or even want certain things, such as a new cell phone. (See the flowchart on page 6.)

- *Refuse*: Say no to things you disagree with, rather than just going along with them. Decide for yourself and don't be a slave to trends.

- *Renew*: Choose renewable resources when you can. Learn about and look for symbols on paper and wood that help you do this.

...and one extra R

Respect, as in "respect your environment," both globally and locally. You and your friends can take the lead by taking care of your neighborhood environment. For example, you can make sure:

- You never drop litter.
- You clean up after your pet if it relieves itself in a public place.
- You pick up any litter you see in your neighborhood.

Eco-song playlist

You could make a playlist of your favorite songs with a green theme. Search for "eco-songs playlist" online and you will find plenty of ideas. One classic on the web lists is "Big Yellow Taxi" by Joni Mitchell. It begins and ends "They paved paradise, put up a parking lot." Look through your collection and list some good eco-friendly songs to share green ideas with your friends.

Freecycle

"Changing the world one gift at a time" is the slogan of the Freecycle network, which has nearly 9 million members around the world. This successful nonprofit movement is all about reuse and, as it says, "keeping good stuff out of landfills." You could use the network to give away unwanted stuff and get stuff for free from others in the same way. Visit www.freecycle.org.

Thinking big...

The way you approach a green lifestyle can combine big and small thinking. The big issue concerns the enormous environmental problems facing the planet. After all, that is why it is important for all of us to go green. Many documentaries, such as *An Inconvenient Truth*, narrated by former vice-president Al Gore, have made people think about climate change for the first time. Many viewers do not find this easy, because it is such an overwhelming problem.

Imagine the polar ice caps melting, sea levels rising, and cities facing the threat of major flooding. These are the big concerns that make us think.

...and small

It is tempting to think, "Well, there's nothing I can do to prevent polar ice from melting, so what's the point in bothering?" But that would be missing the point. None of us can solve the enormous problems, but we all have the power to make a small difference with every green choice we make. Imagine you were cheering on a sports team. Your voice on its own might not be heard, but a whole crowd of voices can have a powerful effect.

This boat, called *Plastiki*, is made of 12,500 reclaimed plastic bottles—a big reuse and recycle campaign! In 2010, its crew sailed across the Pacific Ocean from San Francisco, California, to Sydney, Australia.

Don't get greenwashed!

Some companies tend to exaggerate their green credentials. The deceptive use of green claims is called **greenwashing**, and the environmental group Greenpeace is so concerned about this problem that it runs a special web site (stopgreenwash.org), where you can see examples. In 2011, they claimed that several U.S. airlines advertised that they were "flying cleaner," while at the same time the airlines' lawyers were doing their best to stop new anti-pollution programs.

Being green: Summing up

- Being "green" means being environmentally friendly.
- There are good personal and global reasons why we should all care about the environment.
- Calculate and reduce your carbon footprint.
- Reduce, reuse, recycle, rethink, refuse, renew, and respect.
- Think big (global warming) and small (every little bit helps).
- Watch out for greenwashing.

Green Options at Home

You probably spend most of your free time at home, so that is where the idea of eco-leisure really comes in. Perhaps you are already much greener than you think? Some of the ideas here may be so simple that you started doing them long ago. Others may be new to you and provide inspiration on how to make your home life more environmentally friendly. Some depend on cooperation from your parents or guardians, who, after all, pay the bills. It will be up to you to convince them that your suggestions make sense.

Waking up to energy use

We all use electrical energy from the moment we get up. In cold weather, your central heating probably wakes up before you. The heating system is not your responsibility, but one day it will be. Your parents will welcome any attempts you make to save money. So, if you get out of bed and feel the cold, do not run straight to the thermostat to turn it up. Put on a sweater instead! It is up to your parents to think about insulating your home properly, using an **energy-efficient** furnace, and so on. But you can help by simply saving energy. You could even do some exercises to warm yourself up on cold mornings!

There is more than one way to get some exercise at home! You can have fun burning your own energy.

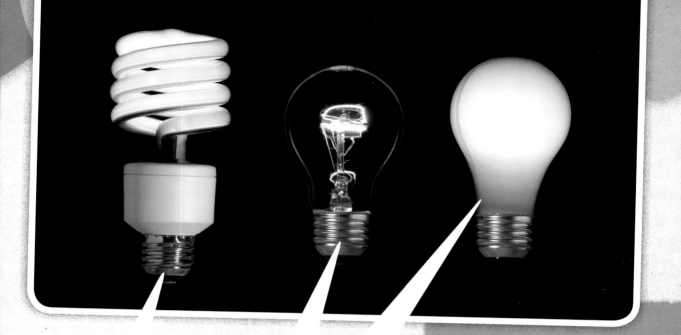

fluorescent lightbulb   incandescent lightbulbs

Eco impact

If you have any old-fashioned incandescent lightbulbs in your house, be aware that at least 90 percent of the energy they use is given off as heat (not light)! So, persuade your parents to buy newer fluorescent bulbs that use five times less energy and last up to twelve times longer.

Why bother to save energy?

Much of the energy we use, including electricity, comes from fossil fuels. We are using more of these fuels than ever before, and one day they will run out. These fuels also pollute the atmosphere with waste gases when they are burned to give off energy. Renewable sources of energy are much better for the environment, and some electricity companies supply power only from these. They include **biomass**, geothermal, solar, water, and wind power.

Switch off

Now, here's an obvious idea when it comes to saving energy: turn lights off when they are not being used! When you head for the bathroom, remember to switch off lights in the bedroom. By the way, has anyone ever told you that turning lights off (and then on again) uses more energy than leaving them on? Well, it is not true, so don't try to use that old excuse!

Bathroom routine

Do you ever leave the faucet running when you brush your teeth? If so, you have an easy way to improve your green account! Turning the faucet off while you brush could save almost 2,000 gallons (9,000 liters) of water a year. The same applies in the kitchen: don't let the water run more than it needs to. In regions of the world where water is always short, people would never dream of washing vegetables under running water—they use a container instead. It is a habit, not a chore they always have to think about. By the way, hand-washing dishes typically uses about 6.6 gallons (30 liters) of water. If the dishes are rinsed under a running faucet, the total can rise to 13.2 gallons (60 liters).

One study discovered that teenagers use 21 gallons (95 liters) of water for their shower! That is almost as much water as taking a bath (see below).

Showers versus baths

Most people will tell you that a shower uses less water than a bath. But of course it depends how big the bath is and how long you shower for! A medium-sized bath holds about 33 gallons (150 liters) of water, and let's say we fill it two-thirds full, and so use about 22 gallons (100 liters) of water per bath. The average shower uses about 2.2 gallons (10 liters) of water per minute, so if you shower for 5 minutes, you use 11 gallons (50 liters)— half the bathwater. But surveys show that people tend to take between 8 and 10 minutes for their shower, so it is all about keeping your time under the shower short.

Saving water every day

If you showered for one minute less every day, you would save about 800 gallons (3,650 liters) of water a year. You would also save the energy that would be used to heat that water. One way to cut your time down is to turn the shower off while you shampoo your hair. For one week, time yourself every day. You may be surprised when you see how long your shower routine is! Another tip is to persuade your parents to have a flow restrictor fitted to the shower. This cheap piece of equipment can reduce the flow per minute to 0.9–1.3 gallons (4–6 liters)—half the normal amount—and you still get a good shower!

Your shower timings might give you a surprise. Set yourself a 5-minute target.

Day	Minutes
Mon	7
Tue	6
Wed	6 ½
Thu	6
Fri	5 (success!)
Sat	5 ½
Sun	6

Why bother to save water?

Water is a precious resource, which all living things need to live. As the world's population grows, more parts of the world are suffering from "water stress." Many **developing countries** are very short of fresh drinking water. The average American uses 126 gallons (575 liters) a day. In poor parts of Africa, many people have to live on less than 9 gallons (40 liters) per day. The average in Mozambique is 0.9 gallon (4 liters).

Computer time

Chances are, one of the first things you look at in the morning is your computer. You will probably look at it for several hours during the day. A U.S. survey from 2010 found that 8- to 18-year-olds spend more than 7½ hours surfing the Internet, playing video games, or watching TV each day. And most are multitaskers. Forty percent use another medium, such as a music player or a cell phone, while on their computer. They also spend about an hour and a half texting each day.

Multitasking by using two or three devices at the same time can use up a lot of electricity.

Watch out for stand-by

Do you usually leave your computer or other appliances on? Well, that really is a waste of energy, because stand-by mode often uses 6–20 **watts** of electricity. Look at these figures for the amount of watts used by a typical laptop in different modes:

Device	Watts
fully on, charging	44.3
fully on, charged	29.5
sleep	15.8
stand-by (off)	8.9
power supply only	4.4

This band is playing in a park in San Diego, California, in celebration of International Earth Day. This special green date comes around every year on April 22.

Laptop versus desktop

The average laptop uses up to 85 percent less energy than a desktop computer. Even on "idle" or "sleep" mode, laptops are far more energy-efficient, using about a tenth of the power of a desktop. Here are some tips to save computer energy:

- Switch your computer off when you are not using it. Powering down could lengthen a laptop's life.
- Use the power management function on your computer (via the control panel or system preferences).
- Turn the monitor off whenever you can. It uses about two-thirds of the energy needed to power the computer.
- Plug your laptop in rather than using the battery when you can, to reduce energy lost through battery charging and discharging.
- Don't rush to upgrade to the latest computer with a faster processor—it will use more electricity.

Eco impact

You can drive almost 2 miles (3.2 kilometers) in an electric car or make 12 mugs of tea with the energy needed to download the average album. This is still up to 80 percent more energy-efficient than buying a CD. However, if you decide to burn a CD of your new album, this would be nearly three times as energy-wasteful as buying the album on a CD in the first place.

Online shopping

Which do you think are greener—retail stores or online stores? According to research, an average trip to a shopping center produces more than 9 pounds (4 kilograms) of CO_2, compared with a delivery vehicle amount of about 6 ounces (180 grams). Per product, e-commerce warehouses use about one-sixteenth of the energy used by retail stores. However, there is a downside: goods bought online need strong packaging, which takes energy to make and creates waste.

Here are a few tips to make online shopping greener:

- Go online only for products that you cannot get locally.
- Try to buy from one e-seller, saving on packaging and delivery.
- Stick to e-retailers that state they use recycled packaging.
- Use non-express delivery services.
- Download music, movies, and books—there is no packaging or shipping. Just make sure it is legal!

Technotrash

So, what should you do with old CDs, jewel cases, and the hardware your parents bought to play them on? You may have heard of gardeners using strings of old CDs to scare birds away. There are lots of other craft projects for which they might be useful. However, there are companies that will take this kind of thing—called technotrash or **e-waste**—and dispose of it properly or, even better, recycle it. Just search online for "recycle CDs," "recycle technotrash," or "recycle e-waste" and you will find lots of possibilities.

This is an unusual wall hanging. How many more ways to reuse your old CDs can you think of?

Recycled glitter ball

Here's a good way to put your old CDs to reuse. Make a glittering decoration or disco ball!

You will need:

lots of old CDs; glue; nylon thread or string; a sphere (you could use an old plastic ball, a round paper lantern or light shade, or you could make your own papier mâché sphere, as shown below)

Method:

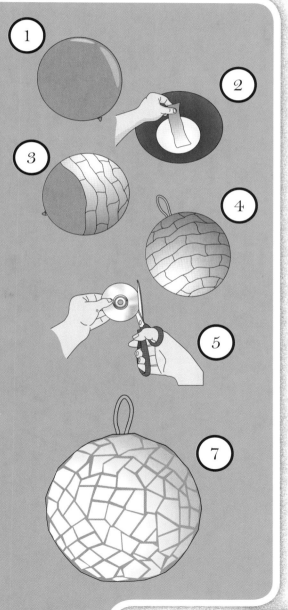

1. Blow up a round balloon. To make papier mâché, tear old newspaper into strips. Mix one cup of flour with two cups of water until the mixture is smooth.

2. Coat each paper strip with paste, removing any lumps with your fingers.

3. Cover the balloon with one layer of strips in one direction and a second layer in the other direction. Stick on at least four layers and leave to dry for two days.

4. Pierce a hole in the top and push a piece of knotted string into it for a hanger. Secure it with strong glue or tape.

5. Wear goggles to protect your eyes from splinters. Cut the CDs into small shapes. Make sure there are no pets or small children around who may accidentally swallow the pieces, and be careful not to cut or scratch yourself.

6. Glue the CD pieces mirror-side out all around the ball. Start from the center and fit the shapes in as you go.

7. Hang the glitter ball up and shine a light at it to make it sparkle. If you use a ball, glue on nylon thread for hanging up before sticking on the CDs.

Your most prized possession?

In 2011, a survey of British teenagers found that three-quarters of them said their most prized possession was their cell phone. So, it is not really surprising to discover their greatest fear was having their phone confiscated by their parents as punishment. Fifteen percent of the teenagers questioned admitted this regularly happened to them. They also admitted the main reason for confiscation was overspending their phone budget. A U.S. survey discovered that teenagers make or receive an average of only six cell calls every day. However, they send or receive 96 text messages (quite a lot!). No wonder the cell is a teenager's most prized possession!

Solar chargers

It is obvious to anyone that it is greener to use rechargeable batteries than the single-use kind. Try to use them for all your portable devices. Rechargeables are built into cell phones, but did you know there are also solar chargers on the market, for use with your cell, as well as your iPod or laptop? The charger builds up a store of electricity from its solar cells when left in the light. You then plug your device into the charger when you are low on power. The charger itself is small and portable, so you can take it with you on vacation or simply when you are out and about.

This solar-powered charger is being used to load up a cell phone battery.

The world now has more than 5.6 billion cell phones, and some are greener than others.

How green is your cell?

You may have heard horror stories about "conflict minerals," especially in Central Africa, being used in the manufacture of cell phones. The sale of these minerals may be used to fund wars and may result in serious human rights abuses. There are campaigns you can join to protest against this problem, which seems to affect all cell phone manufacturers. There are other issues, too, such as the use of toxic chemicals, problems of e-waste, and poor working conditions in factories.

Greenpeace International publishes an online Guide to Greener Electronics, which ranks leading cell phone, TV, and PC manufacturers on their impact on the environment, production techniques, and attempts to make their operations more **sustainable**. The guide also gives points for energy efficiency, use of recycled plastic, and many other factors. To check out your brand, go to www.greenpeace.org and search for "guide to greener electronics."

Being green: Summing up
- Switch off lights and switch to fluorescent lightbulbs.
- Save water in the shower.
- Reduce energy use by not using the stand-by mode.
- Laptops are greener than desktops.
- Online shopping is green, but it has disadvantages, too.
- Find ways to deal with technotrash and e-waste.
- Use a solar charger for your cell phone.

Fun with Friends

It is not always easy to keep up your green credentials with your friends. You may have to convince some of them that green ideas are worth pursuing. A lot of the time you spend together involves modern technology and gadgets, but there are many ways you and your friends can use modern technology in a greener way.

Conducting a survey

You spend a lot of time with your friends, and you probably all have similar problems and worries. Like you, they may be interested in trying to be greener in their free time. But have you ever discussed green issues together? If not, you should try it. The next time you get together, suggest you spend half an hour throwing out ideas and sharing experiences. Another way to do this would be to carry out a survey:

- Have you tried one of the new solar-powered phone chargers?

- Do you have any special ways of saving energy at home?

- Can you think of a project that we could do together to help our local community?

Since video games are interactive, you can always play them on your own. But playing with other gamers can be even more fun.

Video games

In the United States, video game systems use enough electricity to power a city the size of San Diego, California. That is a great deal of energy, and according to the U.S. National Resources Defense Council, turning off game consoles when not in use could save individuals almost $100 a year. The council's study found the greenest system is Nintendo Wii, which uses less power than its competitors. Here are some tips to green up your gaming:

- Turn off the console when it is not in use. Idle machines use almost as much energy as active ones.
- Activate the power-save mode. This is often buried in the menus and very difficult to find, but it is well worth the effort.
- Don't watch movies on your game system. This can use five times more power than watching them on players such as Blu-Ray.

Electronic versus paper communication

Which is greener, an e-mail or a letter? Here are some issues:

- Paper is from a renewable source (managed forests). Computers are made from nonrenewable materials (oil, metals, and minerals) that have to be mined and refined.
- It takes a lot more energy to manufacture a computer than it does paper, but they are difficult to compare like for like.
- Manufacturing both causes acid rain and water pollution.
- It is much easier to recycle paper, and more people do so. E-waste, including old computers, is a big problem.

If you already own a computer, then it is greener to send e-mails. But if you look at the bigger picture, then paper is the greener option. In any case, avoid doubling up—do not

It's eco-party time!

The next time you throw a party at home for your friends, make it a green party. Start by sending e-vites (e-mailed invitations) instead of buying cards, envelopes, and postage stamps. Many charities offer an e-card service, and you could consider donating the money saved to a good cause. You will be promoting the charity to your friends.

Eco-friendly food

What sort of food are you going to offer your guests? You definitely want it to be environmentally friendly, so the first thing you could think about is **organically** grown food. The word *organic* describes farming methods that do not use **pesticides** or artificial fertilizers on crops or chemical treatments on animals. Foods that are labeled organic must come from land that has been farmed in this natural way for at least two years. **Organic farming** is definitely greener, providing healthy food and using less energy. Experts have calculated that industrial farming can mean burning 10 calories of fossil fuels to produce one calorie of food.

When you buy fruit from your local farmers' market, you know it has not traveled too far. If you are not sure, ask where the produce has come from.

Go local

If you buy your food at local stores, you can avoid building up **food miles**. This is the distance food travels from where it is grown to where it is consumed. Research in the United States shows that produce from local farmers within a state travels an average of 56 miles (90 kilometers), while out-of-state food travels more than 25 times farther. Try to buy from local stores or farmers' markets and avoid supermarkets, which buy food from long distances away. At the same time, you will be supporting members of your local community, whether you live in a big city or a small town. If we do not support our local stores, they may close. Then we will have no choice but to give our money to the large national and international retailers.

Waste and precycling

The best way to avoid waste is to precycle, which means pre-recycling or preventing recycling. Do this by avoiding packaging and disposable items. Here are some precycling tips:

- Take reusable bags to go shopping (see page 5).
- Buy foods with the least amount of packaging or none at all. Fruits and vegetables can be loose rather than wrapped in plastic.
- If there has to be packaging, check that it is recycled (look for the special symbol shown on the right).
- Don't buy disposable items such as paper plates or napkins.
- Avoid expanded polystyrene packaging, which is not accepted by many recyclers and is the most difficult material to break down in landfills.
- Cardboard, aluminum, steel, glass, and plastic containers can be recycled more easily.

This recycling symbol is used and recognized around the world. You will find it on all sorts of products.

Dispose of disposable dishes

At your party, use regular dishes, metal cutlery, and cloth napkins—even though it will mean a lot more cleaning up afterward! If your household has a dishwasher, set it on economy wash with a full load and it will use less hot water than washing dishes by hand.

Eating out

For your own or someone else's birthday, you and your friends might want to go out for a meal. To make sure you choose somewhere that shares your wish to be green, you will need to do some research. You can look at the restaurant's web site, if it has one. But there is no substitute for going on foot or by bike and having a look at the place itself. Many food web sites and magazines also list restaurants that are particularly green and serve organic food.

You can eat with your friends at a local pizzeria. If you want to check out the restaurant's green credentials, look for the points listed on the next page.

Green stars

The Green Restaurant Association was founded in San Diego, California, in 1990. It says that it aims "to provide convenient and cost-effective tools to help the restaurant industry reduce its harmful impact on the environment." The GRA, now based in Boston, Massachusetts, visits restaurants and awards stars according to scores against seven different test categories. The tests are for:

- water efficiency
- waste reduction and recycling
- sustainable furnishings and building materials
- sustainable food (from organic and local family farms)
- energy use
- use of disposables
- chemical and pollution reduction.

The GRA lists restaurants and their stars at its web site, www.dinegreen.com.

Checking out credentials

Check out the credentials of your local restaurants. A small restaurant was given a green award for offering these advantages:

- Up to 80 percent of waste is recycled and the restaurant is testing new waste management strategies.
- It used reusable cutlery and eco-friendly takeout containers.
- Packaging is sent back to the supplier for reuse when possible.
- A choice of serving sizes is offered, creating less food waste.
- Herbs are grown on site.
- It is open to the public, schools, and trainee chefs as an educational resource.
- Water is purified on site.
- Green electricity (from renewable sources) is used.
- All food is bought from local producers.

There are lots of ways for restaurants to gain a good green rating.

Green your Halloween

You could always come up with green ideas for special parties and gatherings. Here are a few green ideas for Halloween:

- For your costume, reuse clothing you already own or visit a local thrift store for inspiration.
- If you decide to use makeup, make sure it's nontoxic.
- For candy and treats, look for fair trade and/or organic chocolate.
- In addition to carving faces in pumpkins, roast the seeds and use the flesh to make delicious pumpkin soup. You will find lots of good recipes in cookbooks and online.

Outdoor activities

In addition to parties and special events, there are lots of green outdoor activities you can do with your friends. At the same time, you can help your local community.

You can make quite an impression with a simple old sheet!

Pedal power

If you enjoy cycling with your friends, maybe you could do more pedaling on your own, too? You could use a bike for riding to school, visiting friends, and running errands. You will need to get a good helmet, front and rear lights, and a reflective vest. Another good green idea is bicycle sharing programs. You can rent a bike from a special station. These programs have been used in cities such as Minneapolis, Minnesota, Boston, Massachusetts, and London, England.

Biking...

The great thing about cycling is there are no **greenhouse gases** involved. Bikes cause no pollution. They also take up very little space, so there is plenty of room on the road or on the cycle path. When you cycle instead of getting a ride in a car, you are doing your part for the planet. You are helping yourself, too, because cycling is a great way to stay fit. It is also a good way to make new friends. But there are a few things you should think about:

- Learn how to mend a flat tire yourself and use a hand pump, rather than a device that uses electricity.
- When it gets dark, use a rechargeable light.
- Don't bother with flashy aerodynamic cycling outfits. But safety must always come first, so wear reflective clothing.
- You don't really need sports drinks and energy bars, either; everyday organic food and drinks will do. Water is the best thing you can drink to stay hydrated.

If you want to see how green your bike rides are, take the quiz on: sierraclub.org/howgreen/bikeride.

This young man from Rosario, Argentina, made his own bike frame out of bamboo, an environmentally friendly material (see page 34).

...and hiking

All kinds of hiking can also be green and can be a lot of fun to do with friends. If you go out hiking, there are certain rules to follow (see page 44). The most important green rule is to leave no trace of your presence. Of course, you can also have a lot of green fun enjoying a walk in your town or city, where the same rules apply.

Local projects

You could have more green fun with your friends by taking part in local environmental projects. Most local governments have a whole range of environmental projects underway at any one time. They are always looking for young volunteers to help carry out these programs. For some, you might need the approval of your parents or another adult. Such projects are also a great way to make friends with other like-minded people. Local projects will obviously require little travel. They might involve surveys, questionnaires, or passing on information to raise awareness of environmental topics. These might cover the benefits of recycling, the problems of littering, or ways in which to improve or restore local **habitats**. You can get advice from nonprofit organizations such as the Newton Eco-Team Project (greendecade. org).

Amsterdam, in the Netherlands, is a cycling city. It has 600,000 bikes, many for rent, and you can ride along 250 miles (400 kilometers) of special cycle paths.

Local science survey

In 2011, two British universities asked for volunteers to help with a survey of their local horse chestnut (or conker) trees. This kind of tree is being damaged by the caterpillars of leaf-mining moths. The insects came originally from southern Europe and were first discovered in Britain in 2002. The volunteers were asked to make a survey of their local trees and report on the damage. They were also encouraged to collect leaves, put them in plastic bags, and then see how many moths eventually emerged. This is the sort of project for which a group of committed teenagers is ideal. You would be helping scientists and the local community as well as learning about ecology.

Your own ideas

Do you or your friends have any ideas about local environmental issues? You might not have thought about this before, but you could begin by getting some friends together to talk about your local community. The issues you raise will vary according to your location, and whether you live in the middle of a big city or in the country. You could do some online research before meeting your friends, so that you can put forward ideas.

These students from a school in Michigan are planting vegetation to help stabilize a river bank. This is an excellent example of a successful local environmental project.

Check out what's going on

Your local government's web site will probably list the green projects that are already underway in your area. This will put you in touch with existing projects. Many governments also have a regular e-mail newsletter that will keep you informed of work in progress. There may be an online directory, which will help you find other volunteer groups near you. You can be sure that other groups will be pleased to hear from you, especially if you are offering help. For example, you may be planning to clean up and de-litter the banks of a local pond or stream. Other groups may have experience and could help you with planning by pointing out problems you may encounter.

Green sports equipment and clothing

If you want to become greener in the sport you play, you can make a contribution by making sure that your equipment and clothing are as environmentally friendly as possible. For example, you can buy skateboards, snowboards, and surfboards made of bamboo or hemp. The fibers from these plants are sometimes called **eco-fibers**. Both plants are fast-growing, need no chemical pesticides, and require less water than other plants. So, they can be farmed in a more sustainable way than trees or other woody plants. Their eco-fibers can also be used for making clothing. In addition to these materials, for all your outdoor sports you can wear clothes such as underwear and fleece made from recycled materials; recycled rubber-soled walking boots; and organic cotton clothes.

Make your sports activities greener by thinking about what you wear and what you use. For some green tips on winter vacations, see page 46.

From (green) tee to green

Do you enjoy golfing, or are you thinking of taking up golf? You may know that many environmentalists have criticized the game. Critics say that golf courses take up too much land, changing the landscape and reducing **biodiversity**. They need huge amounts of water and are often treated with fertilizers and pesticides. But things are changing. In the United States, a project called the Golf & the Environment Initiative, in partnership with the U.S. Golf Association, is raising environmental awareness. It has a list of eco-friendly golf courses.

Making water sports safer

As a result of human actions, our oceans and lakes are becoming polluted and dangerous. So, people involved with water sports such as surfing are trying to make a difference. They are forming organizations that work to achieve clean, safe water free from sewage pollution, toxic waste, and plastic litter. They report any pollution they find to the health authorities, help to clean up beaches, and hold educational talks to spread the green word. The American Surfrider Foundation, based in California, is one such group. Visit its web site at www.surfrider.org.

You and your friends can organize your own fun game of baseball or softball. Or you could join a club to work on your skills more seriously.

Being green: Summing up

- Survey and learn about your friends' green ideas.
- Save energy on your video games.
- Paper communication still has a lot going for it.
- Look out for eco-friendly, local food.
- Go biking and hiking, which are great green activities and a good way to make friends.
- Take part in local environmental programs.
- Check whether your sports are green.

Traveling Green

Traveling can have an enormous environmental impact, so you should always consider how and why you go to places. For local trips, you can decide to go on foot or by bike. For longer journeys or vacations, the transportation you use might not be your decision. Your parents, adult relatives, or friends may decide for you. But it is still important to know the facts, which might help you come up with ideas for greener family vacations.

The green way to go

Traveling by train is usually best in terms of low carbon emissions. A bus is about the same. Car travel depends very much on the number of passengers. Four or more people can sometimes compete with traveling by diesel train over the same distance.

You can be aware of green travel and still have a great family vacation.

What about flying? Well, we all have to accept that aircraft are extremely polluting. They emit gases and particles high in the atmosphere, which is particularly damaging. They emit water vapor, which is also a greenhouse gas. It has been estimated that aircraft contribute 3 percent of all greenhouse gases from human sources. This is set to rise to 5 percent by 2050. Flying counts for 40 percent of global tourism emissions. In 2008, an aviation conference predicted that total CO_2 pollution from aircraft could double by 2025. Nevertheless, we must accept that flying to a destination is sometimes the only practical or even affordable option. But we can all aim to look for alternatives when possible.

Figures for a journey

These figures show the amount of CO_2 produced by different types of transportation for different numbers of passengers. There is a low and high estimate for each, calculated by Forum for the Future, a nonprofit organization. The figures are higher than those sometimes quoted by transportation companies, because they include emissions all the way from mining the fuel to the fuel tank in the vehicle.

The first three sets of figures assume a certain average number of total passengers in the plane, train, or bus. The car figure is figured out for the vehicle, so it gets more efficient with more passengers. The figures are for a journey of about 1,000 miles (1,600 kilometers)—roughly the same distance as New York City to Minneapolis, Minnesota.

	passengers	lb. (kg) carbon/ low estimate	lb. (kg) carbon/ high estimate
By air	1	608 (276)	937 (425)
	2	1,217 (552)	1,874 (850)
	4	2,434 (1,104)	3,748 (1,700)
By train	1	115 (52)	483 (219)
	2	229 (104)	966 (438)
	4	459 (208)	1,931 (876)
By road: bus	1	112 (51)	408 (185)
	2	225 (102)	814 (369)
	4	450 (204)	1,627 (738)
By road: car	1	666 (302)	1,340 (608)
	2	666 (302)	1,340 (608)
	4	666 (302)	1,340 (608)

One of the advantages of train travel is that you can read or use your computer in comfort.

Air travel: What do you think?

What is your opinion about air travel? This is a tricky issue, and you could discuss it with your friends when you talk about going green. Here are some questions for you to think about:

- Do you think governments should restrict international air travel? If so, how would they do this? Should vacationers be discouraged from making long journeys? What about business travelers? What about people with families who live in other countries?

- The International Air Transport Association (IATA) is the governing body that regulates air travel. It says that its aim is "to achieve carbon neutral growth in the medium term and to build a plane that produces no emissions within 50 years." Airlines have improved fuel efficiency and reduced CO_2 emissions by 14 percent over the past 10 years. They say they have reduced fuel use and CO_2 emissions per passenger kilometer by 70 percent compared to the 1970s. Do you think more should be done?

- Do you agree with a carbon tax on airlines? In 2012, the European Union (EU) introduced a charge on flights based on their carbon emissions. The tax applies to all airlines landing planes in EU countries, but Chinese airlines refused to pay the tax and risked fines. Do you think the tax is a good idea?

- Airlines will surely pass increased costs, such as a carbon tax, on to passengers. Maybe air travel is too cheap, anyway? Compared with other costs, air travel is much less expensive than 25 years ago. Given what we now know about the problems of global warming, is this right? What do you and your friends think? You could debate it!

Air travel and local economies

In the United States, air travel is extremely important to the economy. In 2008, 58 million international travelers visited the United States, and these international travelers spent $110.4 billion (not including airfares). This is true in many other parts of the world, including in poorer countries that can offer beautiful beaches and historic sites to tourists. Does this affect your opinion about air travel, and whether or not it should be limited?

Air travel is fast and convenient. We have become very used to the option of flying. But do we rely on it too much? Is it time to rethink our attitudes toward planes?

Greener fuels

Greener fuels have been developed for cars and buses. These include **biofuels** (such as ethanol), electricity, and other power sources. Hybrid cars combine a gasoline engine with an electric motor. At slow speeds, the car runs on electricity. On faster roads, it switches to gasoline and recharges the electric battery. One of the most interesting developments is hydrogen-powered fuel cells, which generate electricity to power vehicles. This is a green solution, because all that is needed are hydrogen and oxygen, with water as a harmless by-product. The problem scientists still have to solve is that it takes a lot of energy to split hydrogen from other substances.

Two-wheeled eco-carrier

Do you sometimes leave your bike at home because you have a lot of things to carry? Well, you can make your bike more useful by turning it into a kind of eco-vehicle. You could carry your load in a basket or handlebar bag at the front. The basket could be made of wicker or wire mesh, and you could use the mounting point for your front light. Or you could fit a saddle bag under your seat, with a quick-release mechanism, so that you can get the things you need in a flash.

Alternatively, you could fit special bags called panniers or rack bags. They are best fitted in balanced pairs to a rack over your front or rear wheels. They can carry lots of stuff and come in a range of designs and fabrics, from the traditional to the high-tech and waterproof, which are useful in all weathers. These bike extras could go a long way to making your life greener. They also take the strain off your back, so you do not have to carry a large backpack.

Here is an excellent example of an eco-vehicle! This rider is carrying panniers on both front and back wheels, as well as using bags attached to the seat and to the handlebars.

Let's share

If you have to get a regular ride to school or anywhere else, try to make sure the car is as full as possible. A car with a driver and four passengers is much greener than four cars with one passenger each! You could talk to your parents and friends about starting up a carpooling program. Adults can take turns driving, and they will soon see how much time and money they save. At the same time, you will be doing your part to save the planet a few exhaust emissions.

If your parents or other adults are interested, there are also lots of carpooling programs with dedicated web sites. In some cities, there are special "carpool" lanes, so that eco-friendly carpoolers have an easier, faster journey.

Going public

Using buses and trains helps reduce the volume of traffic on the roads, reducing congestion and helping you limit your carbon footprint. If there are twenty people on the bus, it is the same as five of the shared cars we mentioned. Many towns and cities now have integrated systems, so you can travel on buses, trams, and trains on one ticket. Encourage your car-bound friends to join you on public transportation.

Being green: Summing up
- Travel on foot or by bike whenever you can.
- Compare different kinds of transportation for eco-friendliness.
- Travel by train, bus, or tram for longer journeys.
- Should we think about putting more carbon tax on aircraft?
- Greener fuels and hybrid cars will help.
- Turn your bike into an eco-vehicle by adding accessories.
- Encourage adults to share cars and journeys.
- Use public transportation.

Eco-Vacations

The International Ecotourism Society defines ecotourism as "responsible travel to natural areas that conserves the environment and improves the well-being of local people." Environmentalists are very concerned that tourists should travel responsibly because, no matter how hard they try, it is difficult for them not to leave their mark on their destination. When we are tourists, we all inevitably create waste and pollution. The problem is growing all the time. In 1970, there were about 175 million international tourists. By 2010, this number had grown to more than 940 million.

Responsible tourism ensures that extreme sports and other activities do not harm the environment.

Responsible tourism

When we go on vacation, we all want to be responsible. What does that actually mean? Will it help us to be green, too? At a conference in Cape Town, South Africa, representatives from all over the world drew up guidelines in a declaration. They said that responsible tourism:

- needs to minimize negative environmental and social impacts
- generates greater economic benefits for local people
- involves local people in decisions that affect their lives
- makes positive contributions to **conservation**
- provides understanding of local cultural and social issues
- provides access for physically challenged people
- engenders respect between tourists and local people.

Staying in a green hotel

If your family plans to stay in a hotel, there are ways you can make it a greener vacation. The U.S. Green Hotel Initiative helps travelers ask for environmentally friendly services when they check in. For example, a Guest Request Card asks the hotel to replace toiletries only when they are used up. You could take cards like this (available from www.ceres.org) or make your own list. No matter what you choose, it is best to speak to staff members at the hotel when you arrive.

In theory, the hotel owners should be pleased, because you are asking for things that will save them money. Some hotels have their own cards. You could make your own list with your parents or the adults you are traveling with. What points would you like to make?

☐ Do not replace sheets and towels every day

☐ Keep the air conditioning turned down

☐ Recycle plastic bottles and paper

Saving on resources

When you are away, you can save on resources just as you do at home. In your hotel, or wherever else you are staying, try to make sure you:

- turn off lights and other things that use electricity when you leave
- don't waste water
- use only the toiletries you need
- reuse towels, bathrobes, and sheets until they need washing
- keep the rest of your laundry to a minimum.

Can you add some other points?

An eco-festival or eco-fair is a great destination for a day out. You can have fun and pick up some green ideas at the same time.

Off to the wilderness

We all know that trips to explore nature, including hiking and camping, are a lot of fun. We also know there have to be special green rules so that the natural areas stay green for us and others to enjoy. Imagine standing at a beautiful spot to admire the view and seeing out of the corner of your eye a cigarette butt, candy wrapper, or piece of toilet paper. View ruined!

Here are some basic tips to follow in nature:
- Leave no trace, so that you have a natural habitat to return to. With a little planning, it is easier than you think. Take garbage bags so that you do not leave any waste.
- Never leave even the smallest piece of litter. Stuff wrappers in your pockets or backpack.
- Stay on paths. Every time you stray off a path, you create an opening for others to follow, which will eventually widen the trampled area.
- Use unbreakable dishes and utensils rather than disposable paper or polystyrene versions.
- Wash dishes and yourself with non-toxic, **biodegradable** soap.
- Shower and wash dishes using as little water as possible.
- Dump gray water (old dishwater) in designated areas, away from fresh water sources, and not in the bushes.

Keeping Yellowstone beautiful

Yellowstone National Park is a beautiful spot of wilderness located primarily in Wyoming. On its web site (www.nps.gov/yell/planyourvisit/impact.htm), it asks visitors to follow basic steps to minimize their impact:

- Swimming is discouraged in general.
- People must stay at least 100 yards (91 meters) from bears and 25 yards (23 meters) from other wildlife.
- Visitors must leave all natural, historical, and archeological items in place.
- Bikes are not allowed on back-country trails or on boardwalks.

When nature calls

In the United States, all but the most remote camping and hiking areas have public restrooms. For the sake of the environment, you should seek out these facilities rather than relieving yourself elsewhere. Keep an eye out for restrooms and other public facilities as you travel throughout the grounds. Make a note of where to find them later, and plan convenient restroom breaks if you worry that you will end up traveling too far from the facilities. It is also very important to remember to stay on official park land. If you are found walking anywhere else, it is considered trespassing.

In the rare instances when you are far away from public restrooms and need to relieve yourself, find a private spot far away from water sources. Dig a hole at least 15 centimeters (6 inches) deep. Take toilet paper back out with you in a garbage bag or bury it in the hole. Fill the hole back in. Human waste is unsightly and can present a health hazard, so it is important to be responsible.

Can wildlife tourism be green?

Wildlife tourism is an important industry in many countries. It can be green as long as tourists follow the rules. Some tour companies specialize in wildlife vacations, and they will make sure you enjoy yourself and leave the animals and their habitats as you found them. In 2011, a safari tour operator based in Malawi and Zambia was joint overall winner of the Responsible Tourism Award for its excellent work with local African communities. The company runs safari camps in a Zambian National Park that is home to many species of birds and animals.

Watching wild animals in their natural habitat makes for an exciting vacation. Try to find eco options whenever you can.

Winter vacations

One of the likely results of global warming is that high-mountain areas will have less snow and ice. Winter vacations are big business and very popular, however, so many resorts in the world's skiing regions have increased their facilities to make snow and blow it onto the slopes. This uses a lot of energy. Some resorts are greener than others, so if your family is considering a winter-sports vacation, you could research your resort.

Green skiing resorts

- The resort of Lech, in the Austrian Alps, heats about nine-tenths of its ski chalets and hotels from a biomass plant that runs on wood chips and waste. It sends hot water throughout the village. This has replaced individual oil-burning boilers and gotten rid of the air pollution that was spoiling the town.

- The Rockies resort of Vail, Colorado, is using its 300 days of sunshine a year to increase its use of solar panels to generate energy. Vail also claims to have the largest ski-area recycling program in the world, recycling or reusing more than 70 percent of material on the mountain.

There are many miles of cross-country tracks near the Austrian mountain village of Lech. This form of skiing is becoming more popular as downhill slopes become overcrowded.

Non-green "real" snow

- Fact 1: Dubai is a city in the United Arab Emirates. The year-round average temperature is 82 °F (28 °C), with an average high of 102 °F (39 °C) in summer and a low of 54 °F (12 °C) in midwinter.
- Fact 2: Dubai's all-year-round indoor ski resort has an average temperature on the slopes of 28 to 30 °F (-1 to -2 °C). It operates for 1,500 skiers on five runs, with a chair lift and a tow lift. The longest run is 1,312 feet (400 meters) long, with a drop of almost 200 feet (over 60 meters).

These facts seem to contradict one another, but they are both true! The resort has "real" snow, in the sense that cooled water is blown out into a freezing environment, where it crystallizes. This takes an enormous amount of energy. According to one web site (www.treehugger.com), the annual greenhouse gas emissions of Ski Dubai are equivalent to about 900 round-trip flights from Munich, Germany, to Dubai.

Cross-country as well as downhill

Downhill skiing and snowboarding are exhilarating and fun. That is why these sports are so popular. However, the huge numbers of downhillers are putting a lot of strain on mountain habitats, causing erosion and other problems. One way to change this is for more of us to start skiing cross-country rather than downhill. You will need special skis, which could be made of the sustainable timber paulownia. It is tough exercise, because you spend most of your time pushing yourself along flat snow, but it is a lot of fun. Snowboarders or non-skiers could consider snowshoeing instead. This form of winter walking is becoming more popular.

Being green: Summing up

- The tourist industry is growing all the time.
- Responsible tourism and ecotourism are green alternatives to traditional tourism.
- Ask hotels for environmentally friendly services.
- Obey some basic rules in the wilderness when hiking or camping.
- Wildlife tourism can be green.
- Look out for greener winter vacations.
- Try cross-country skiing or snowshoeing.

Summing Up: It's Your Choice!

There are lots of ways in which we can make our leisure time greener. We can all use energy more wisely and efficiently. We can use less water and recycle waste. We can also travel more sensibly, especially by cycling or walking whenever possible. In this book, we have looked at lots of green ideas and practical tips. You may want to follow some up and you may think that some are over the top. But whatever you think, there is no denying that if every one of us tries to be just a little greener, our small actions could add up to big results. It is up to you to help—it's your choice!

The butterfly effect

In 1972, the U.S. scientist Edward Lorenz wrote a paper that asked the question: "Does the flap of a butterfly's wings in Brazil set off a tornado in Texas?" Lorenz was referring to the weather, and his words suggested that a small action in one place can result in big changes somewhere else. We can use this as positive thinking for our small green changes. If millions of people do the same small thing, they can make a real difference.

Replacing the bottle

You could do a small thing with a big effect by giving up bottled water, especially in plastic bottles. In 2011, it was estimated that 38 billion gallons (174 billion liters) of bottled water was sold throughout the world. It takes 8 ounces (162 grams) of oil and 12 pints (7 liters) of water (including power-plant cooling water) to manufacture a 1.7-pint (1-liter) bottle. Experts have calculated that in the United States, the amount of oil needed to make plastic water bottles every year is enough to fuel 100,000 cars for that same period.

Yet in the United States, bottled water generally costs about 1,000 times more than tap water. Many people believe the bottled variety is better for them, but health experts say that tap water is just as good.

If you don't like the taste of tap water, a filter system at home will make a real difference. Then, all you need is a reusable stainless steel bottle to fill up before you leave the house.

Job done?

Your efforts at eco-leisure are worthwhile. But the job is never done, because there are always ways in which we can help our planet more. Think positively and celebrate your achievements. One way to do this is to keep a diary of your green decisions and actions. That way, you will be able to look back later and see what you have achieved—quite a lot! You might even decide to give yourself a small reward to celebrate success. Just make sure it is a green gift!

Quiz

The first 12 questions can be answered by reading this book. The rest may need more research! See page 55 for the answers.

1. **How much bottled water is sold around the world in a year?**
   a) 38 million gallons   c) 38,000 liters
   b) 38 billion gallons   d) 38 liters

2. **Which effect stops heat from escaping from Earth?**
   a) The hothouse effect   c) The greenhouse effect
   b) The Greenpeace effect d) The atmospheric effect

3. **What does CO_2 stand for?**
   a) carbon dioxide   c) carbon monoxide
   b) copper dioxide   d) carbon

4. **Which is not a fossil fuel?**
   a) oil   c) coal
   b) gas   d) wood

5. **Which of these countries' people have the biggest average carbon footprint?**
   a) United Kingdom   c) Australia
   b) Canada   d) United States

6. **Which is not one of the three green Rs?**
   a) reuse   c) recycle
   b) rebel   d) reduce

7. **Making one ton of recycled paper saves how many trees?**
   a) 1   c) 13
   b) 7   d) 17

8. **Which boat was made from reclaimed plastic bottles?**
   a) *Plastiki*   c) *Reclastiki*
   b) *Kontiki*   d) *Titaniki*

9. **How much energy does a fluorescent lightbulb use compared to an incandescent bulb?**
   a) half   c) one-fifth
   b) one-third   d) none

10. **What are athletes in groups like the American Surfrider Foundation against?**
    a) spray   c) sea salt
    b) splashing   d) pollution

11. **What do hybrid cars combine with a gasoline engine?**
    a) diesel motor   c) oil motor
    b) electric motor d) gasoline tank

12. **What is a pannier?**
    a) one of a pair of bags   c) all-around view
    b) small drinking cup   d) set of musical pipes

13. **What percentage of global electricity is produced from renewable sources?**
    a) 50 percent   c) 10 percent
    b) 5 percent   d) 20 percent

14. **How many metal cans can be recycled with the energy needed to make one new one?**
    a) 20   c) 10
    b) 15   d) 5

15. **How much junk mail do Americans receive every year?**
    a) 1 thousand tons   c) 3 million tons
    b) 1 million tons   d) 3 billion tons

16. **Which country produces the most hydroelectricity?**
    a) China   c) Canada
    b) Brazil   d) United States

Glossary

biodegradable able to be broken down naturally by living organisms

biodiversity variety of plants and animals in a particular habitat or the world

biofuel produced from biomass, such as ethanol from sugarcane

biomass organic matter that can be used as a source of energy

carbon footprint measure of the impact you have on the planet, related to the amount of greenhouse gases produced in your daily life through burning fossil fuels for energy

climate change rising temperatures worldwide, caused by the increase of greenhouse gases in the atmosphere that trap the Sun's heat

conservation protecting wild habitats and their plants and animals

degrade to be broken down naturally by living organisms

developing country poor country that is trying to become more advanced economically

disposable made to be thrown away after being used once

eco-fiber material from fast-growing plants, such as bamboo and hemp, that needs no chemical pesticides and relatively little water

emission waste gas produced and given off

energy-efficient using as little energy as possible for a task

e-waste also known as technotrash, it is electronic waste, including old hardware and software such as CDs, old cell phones, and computers

food mile distance that food travels from the point of origin to your table

fossil fuel energy source, such as coal, gas, and oil, that was formed over millions of years from the remains of animals or plants

greenhouse gas one of a group of gases, including carbon dioxide and methane, that contribute to global warming

greenwashing making a misleading claim about the environmental benefits of a product or service

habitat natural home or environment of an animal or plant

landfill area of land where large amounts of waste material are buried under the earth

organic produced without using human-made chemicals

organic farming method of farming that minimizes the use of harmful chemical fertilizers and pesticides. Organic farming is also known as all-natural farming.

pesticide chemical used to kill insects or other organisms that are harmful to crops

renewable source of energy that does not run out

sustainable way of doing something that does not use up too many natural resources or pollute the environment

watt unit of power that measures the rate of using electricity

How much energy per Google search?

Research by a Harvard University scientist shows that performing two Google searches produces the equivalent carbon dioxide of boiling a kettle (0.5 oz., or 15 grams, of CO_2). This figure includes all energy consumption, including that of your computer, the servers hosting the page you are looking at, and the path of the data to your machine.

However, Google disagrees and says its servers produce only 0.007 oz. (0.2 grams) of CO_2 per search. That makes a boiling kettle the same as 750 searches. It says that the following activities amount to the number of Google searches quoted:

Activity	Google searches
Recycled daily newspaper decomposing	850
Producing a glass of orange juice	1,050
Washing a load of dishes in an energy-efficient dishwasher	5,100
A 5-mile (8-kilometer) trip in an average car	10,000
Producing a cheeseburger	15,000

Find Out More

Further reading

Gay, Kathlyn. *Living Green: The Ultimate Teen Guide*. Lanham, Md.: Scarecrow, 2012.

Petronis, Lexi, Karen Macklin, and Jill Buck. *47 Things You Can Do for the Environment*. Boston: Houghton Mifflin Harcourt, 2012.

Savedge, Jenn. *The Green Teen: The Eco-Friendly Teen's Guide to Saving the Planet*. Gabriola Island, B.C.: New Society, 2009.

Sivertsen, Linda, and Tosh Sivertsen. *Generation Green: The Ultimate Teen Guide to Living an Eco-Friendly Life*. New York: Simon Pulse, 2008.

Smith, Sharon J. *The Young Activist's Guide to Building a Green Movement and Changing the World*. Berkeley: Ten Speed, 2011.

Web sites

www.epa.gov/epahome/community.htm#conditions
The Environmental Protection Agency (EPA) has lots of information about protecting the environment.

www.epa.gov/students
This is the part of the EPA site created specifically for students.

globalstewards.org
This web site has a list of ways to reduce, reuse, and recycle.

www.greenpeace.org
Greenpeace is a global organization that campaigns to protect the environment.

www.thedailygreen.com/going-green/6334
This web site offers tips for teens about going green in daily life.

DVDs

An Inconvenient Truth, director Davis Guggenheim (Paramount, 2006)
   This Oscar-winning documentary focused on Al Gore's campaign
   to make the issue of global warming a recognized problem.

Waste Land, director Lucy Walker (New Video, 2011)
   This Oscar-nominated documentary is about turning landfill
   waste into art.

More topics to research

There are many different topics related to green options and leisure.
Here are some more research ideas:

- Teens Turning Green: The California-based, student-led
  movement Teens Turning Green promotes "environmentally
  and socially responsible choices for individuals, schools, and
  communities." It has many projects that you might find
  interesting. You might even want to add some of your own.
  Check out www.teensturninggreen.org.

- Water footprint: A product's water footprint is the volume of fresh
  water used to produce it. This includes the water used in all steps
  of the production chain. You could investigate this, starting with
  food. Visit www.waterfootprint.org.

- City transportation: You could investigate the latest transportation
  programs around the world. Then you could compare them to
  where you live (or your nearest city). You could start by looking at
  the German "Mo'" project: visit mo-bility.com.

Answers to quiz (pages 50–51):
1 b; 2 c; 3 a; 4 d; 5 c; 6 b; 7 d; 8 a; 9 c; 10 d; 11 b; 12 a; 13 d; 14 a;
15 c; 16 b.

Index